Cirque
&
Sky

Kathleen Willard :

Middle Creek Publishing & Audio
2016 • Beulah, CO

Cirque & Sky
Copyright 2016 by Kathleen Willard

Middle Creek Publishing & Audio
9027 Cascade Avenue
Beulah, CO 81023   USA
editor@middlecreekpublishing.com

First Edition
ISBN-13: 978-0-9974200-3-6
ISBN-10: 0997420030

Cover & Book Design:
David Anthony Martin

Cover Photo:
"*Painted Alpine, Copper Basin, Crested Butte, Colorado*" by Stephen Willard

Special Thanks:

Middle Creek Publishing & Audio and ECOCO Books would like to thank
Stephen Willard for his gracious permission to use his photograph on the cover
which contributes to the beauty of this important text.

Also to the Denver Botanical Gardens support of poetry and art for their
commission of broadsides for the poems *Granite & Aspen, Sagebrush & Mica,*
and *Cirque & Sky* (broadsided as *Cirque & Clouds*),

for Stephen

Cirque
&
Sky

(or *A Forest of Wings!*
A Forest of Wings!)

Table of Contents

Granite & Silver

However, our shadows.
However, mountains spit out
scaffolds of an abandoned mine still rich with silver
near the ruined city. Its saloons graced by oil paintings
of corpulent nudes denote a slow decay. Here minerals
shift in the mountain's interior and slender rivers
glide through sleeves of granite. We look at each other
as if it were the first time unveiling
ourselves in this ancient stand of aspens
gleaming gold in the late intaglio of the afternoon sun,
newlyweds despite
the decades, and breathe beautifully into each other's ears.
Some say mountains brim with lost treasure
and dim with a poor man's dissipated dreams. A horse
whinnies somewhere in the valley. Somewhere granite
outcroppings beg for the first spit of snow.

Fracking

These are our apparitions: the sky gleans towards gray, the mouths of caves

filled with quartz call. How long before we are all fluent in earth, our scarring
stops? In an office an engineer imagines molecules deep

past aquifers speak combustion and churn engines
and blasts sand and benzene near the earth's core unloosens eons

of errant natural gas dormant underneath Pawnee Grasslands, an oily ocean
the size of Saudi Arabia still and docile waits

underneath the fossil beds of mastodons and eohippus, the knee-high horses,
first to run wild on the prairie, underneath everyone's water source,

underneath artifacts and evidence of prehistoric campsites
of Folsom man, the Paleo-Indian inhabitants from 12,000 years ago,

underneath the final outpost of the Colorado butterfly plant imperiled globally—
the ocean awaits to be split open

with mobile steel girders and slamming concrete sleeves and fallible into the deepest
recesses of rock to pipe toxic concoctions by roustabouts overworked

and now acrid aluminum air irritates and fire streams from water faucets
in the nearby suburbs. The bonds of our cells unhinge unleashing old

and new contagions and cover-ups the whole procedure deemed safe
while around the clock earth cracks open, we tinker with tectonic plates.

Aspen & Roots

The ocean of trees is our exaltation.
Aspens sigh their last yellow breath
arrange themselves for autumn's
final autopsy. How clear the sky remains.
Thighs of mountains open,
fan out in front of us endlessly available.
Unostracized by proximity

to civilization willows barb wire edges of the slow creek.
The world stills as we collide into each other.
I cannot get close enough to you.
So few enter this mile high kingdom.
Aghast, startled birds flee
and we hike well worn elk trails
hidden by dynasties of aspen.
Scientists assert this stand of trees
is Earth's largest organism,
advancing root by root,
tendrils arch underneath
hard soil to conquer
territories on both sides
of the continental divide.

Uravan, Colorado

Fenced off, nine miles inside barbed wire,
and signs warning of radioactivity and keep out
enter at your own risk, the site closed for all eternity,
after the two hundred and sixty buildings shredded and buried
trees demolished, all
ripped apart with hydraulic shears
even the soil buried in a repository built
to endure the worst storms imaginable in the next
thousand years, the town a player in the nuclear
race. *We are not afraid of uranium here,* the widows say
and take rock samples of uranium from their knick knack
shelves part of their décor and share
the black and white photos of Uravan in its heyday:
their children sliding down hills of radioactive tailings,
used also to lay water pipes, to amend garden soil,
the class pictures in front of the elementary school
and recreation center, the evenings at the Uranium
Drive-In Movie Theatre
near the place where yellowcake was milled,
the soon to be enriched material, a necessary
ingredient for the first atomic bomb.
The acceptable risk lungs crystallizing
from cancer maybe from working deep
in the earth, maybe from smoking,
maybe from the uranium, the radium,
the vanadium coaxed from orange
and neon yellow buttes and quiet mesas.

Cirque & Sky

Eager stowaway ready to board any sailing ship,
I disembark on a different shore,
escape the enslavement of a house.

Yes, our cottonwoods bleed branches in hot winds,
but I could care less witchgrass chokes
yellow daylilies once so lovingly planted.
I long ago abandoned the garden that anchored,

enthralled instead by the genius
of sky point my camera
into clouds intent on enlarging my orbit,
resume study of my archive

of tin globes and old maps highlighting
the routes of barbarians and Arctic explorers,
culling provision lists,
noting their grand intentions.

In this decade, I long for pristine landscapes,
for an incognito, to be sequestered
in a secret cirque blushing alpine flowers,
their almost microscopic petals barely
span my fingertips.
Here, elk have never heard a human voice.

Landscape with Infestation

And so, the new tableau.
The trees have no heart a scientist said
no circulatory system, no savior from drought,
no savior from infestation. Stands of certain
evergreens have no mechanism to stay
the stymied xylem or all embolisms.
No resistance against swarms of cannibals
riding the wind, this silent invasion,
an epidemic assured.
Ips and pine bark—we are all blind
to procedures of bore and breed
their explosion of offspring gnaw
and chisel out of the core
murder all systems of survival.
The mountains brown overnight
and there is nothing to be done.
The forest is a stand of cadavers,
decomposing. The demise of
several species a certainty.
The trees will stop breathing
and beetles in their exoskeletons
and invincible are architects
of the new world.

Hooves & Trout

You taught me to recognize the trees with certainty
to feel bark and decode elm, know birch, declare maple.
Early in our lives we walked into the forest
and you looked down said deer trail
recognizing the glance of their hooves
the almost slight curves, almost obelisks,
and followed traces of broken twigs,
of willows grazed to their resting place
the tall grass molded by curled bodies.
And banged on the riverbank
arousing sleeping trout.

And insisted prepare, the world ablaze
with astonishment and up the trail the air alive,
we chanced on a migration
of butterflies, a species unknown to us,
thousands and thousands hanging on every branch
of every tree, opening and closing their wings,
their tiny flags, the many pages of miniature books.

California Gulch Superfund Site Update,
Leadville, Colorado

It's triage.

We will never renovate this basin of mountains
tattooed by smelters, slag heaps and waste piles.
We are still drawn to the rich lode of minerals
          and fever dreams of fortunes haunt Lost Horse Gulch.

Inside mountains there may be gold still, a vein rich in silver,
but silent mines spit cocktails of toxins
and the legacy of slagheaps obscures vistas
          and leeches cadmium, zinc into the dead zone downriver.

Why are we shocked when waters bruise and spoil?
When a plume of debris disgorges red sludge in rivers? The EPA
rarely pinpoints the next leakage or disaster.
          What else comes to mind when arsenic is mentioned?

A cruel certain death and serial killers? Not neon tailings
or evaporation ponds of orange on the road side, a point of interest
for the curious of our history of scars.
          The truth is buried as always deep in our agency's website~

*of the remedial actions implemented at the California Gulch
Superfund Site, in Lake County, Colorado in the fourth five-year
review indicates that the remedies are protective
          in the short term. However,*

Wasps & Windfalls

Like a mirror, or miracle, the summer's done
with the last hum of the honeybee. The world
relieved as the heat cools, the orchard obese
with plums paper wasps drunk burrow
into ripe flesh. Still winter is almost fictitious
and fumbles, stuns and fails to notice
the last lift of geese on the pond or the trout
frazzled underneath a thin membrane of ice.

Windfalls ferment sustenance for our backyard
fox. I don't understand where summer went,
how our errant ferns yellowed, the fringed edges
browning. How the days quicken, now ash filled,
now the color of dust.

Landscape with Drought

These are the brittle latitudes.
Stands of spruce telegraph thirst into the winds
and soon the siege of beetles consume a city of ancient trees
and incessant waves of infestations shrivel brown the land.
The forest rattles like castanets and shrubs and brush spike
up from hardened dirt.

How can the parched resist the drought as surrender
is never the cure. One spark, one flick then certain infernos
roar and fire fills atmospheres. Ours is the earth
ashed and gray. Ours are the hearts now calcified,
our lungs brim and crumble with blood.
The search for alchemy to stay the singe,

to call down rain from sky stalls.
We measure timid snowpack
keep watch over diminished trees
and wait for dreams of monsoons,
our miracle, to occur. At dusk, on the riverbank
we recite rosaries and toss offerings to appease
any god listening, any god able to gift water.
Will this be our last day
in paradise? We breathe the seldom air
and fortify at a furious pace
against the parched, the dry, the desiccated.

Constellation & Fox

Just this revelation~

The morning begins glorious with the red fox
ravishing our backyard orchard gorging on windfall apples
crisscrossing the *cul-de-sac*, a tame canine
pulling at the leash. What constellation did my fox discover
deep into the night, what clandestine comet
showers witnessed only also by astronomers of insomnia?
The fox slumbers under
our front porch, a strange member of our cat's pride,
and stalks our dreams, this dawn. The world floods
with eerie beauty: stellar jays croon,
the deer guards her speckled twins
graze in our shrubbery.

How can they survive alpine winter,
the orange-vested hunters from out of state?
Migratory, they move to the high country
relying on camouflage
as the forest defoliates all around them.

Landscape with Wildfire

The sky burns orange brocade
smears clouds surreal
singes canyons beyond recognition
a hysteric dancing
from treetop to treetop chars
everything in its wake. So
this is the apocalypse
no longer theoretical.
Every large and small
living thing stampedes to safety~
wrens and honeybees
unable to outrun insistent heat.
Spiders spin
their last webs
as ash avalanches from the sky
and shrouds our house. The invisible
census of the soon incinerated
commences impossible
to complete. Flames jump
fire breaks and even the river
advances as the canyon quivers
and overheats and arroyos crumble.
The news hotshot crews
cannot contain the inferno stuns us
as the fire and heat spawns its own clouds
and fallout. The air sizzles
the wall of smoke marches
through the city
and the fire whirls in the forest
births tornadoes of flames.

Sky & Water

The sun silks mountains and shines granite
into the skin of dolphins pale grey and breaching into the sky one
after another a school testing the new element exuberant
leaving water and leaping into air so expeditionary. The clouds
white foamed waves, a border destabilizes between terra firma
and ethereal air. Even the most miniscule
of elements break down and disperse
Into the atmosphere. The spine
of fourteeners diminish as infinite sky
transubstantiates into infinite sea,
an alchemy imperceptible to the naked eye.

Landscape with Ice Palace, Leadville
Winter Crystal Carnival, 1896

Industrialists took their fortunes and built empires elsewhere
another boondoggle and no atonement and pockmarked
the basin with slag heaps and smelters. The cloud city collapsed
into moonscapes of mine shafts. Wood struts mutate into aliens
fill holding ponds with arsenic and suspect watersheds
from avarice and rusts yields the wet dreams of rich strikes.

Desperadoes scheme the next spectacle
the mountains may yield the new rich strike of ice.
Another vein of wealth, another plunder, the next wonder
of the world and all bets are on a five-thousand-ton ice structure,
its Norman battlements tower 90 feet and dwarf the city.
An ice rink and oyster bar, gaming tables and dance floor,

the town fathers predict an up-tick of tourists. The 1896 Annual
Leadville Winter Crystal Carnival begins and prisms of ice
glow with Edison light bulbs illuminate the five-acre ice structure
and lurid tourists gaze at the centerpieces of wolves taxidermied,
and roses and rainbow trout swim in suspended animation

in walls of ice looking almost alive. In an ice auditorium,
macabre shadow shows depict murders and poetry readings
daily at the *Palace of Living Art and Illusion,* but pickpockets
follow the early spring thaw and tourists left Leadville stampede
and hightail it back home as we do today speed through
the town worried leftover arsenic permeates living tissues

and ancestors of gold and silver rush still bank on festivals,
the reopening of the molybdenum mine its engineers clock
in to cart away half Climax Mountain bagging the Earth's
rarest mineral explained on the menu of the Golden Burro Café.
The timbers for the Ice Palace torn down and rebuilt as barracks
for quickly deputized militia sent to quell a miner's strike.

The Winter Carnival photographs and ephemera archived
evidence of constant boom and bust the town collateral
damage and trailers that should be condemned decades ago,
and storefronts remain empty eternally and any data of calamity
and industrial waste tweaked. The valley lurches into the next century
waits for the benefits of the Ice Palace to materialize.

Mica & Sagebrush

A forest of wings! A forest of wings!
The valley sun-bloodied.
The war was just over
and there was little to do but imagine.
The herd of clouds shroud
the mountains one cluster militant
spills down the pale valley
floor. Our abacus counts
the multitude of horses
and keeps track of many ways
to speak of love. Our tally
could fill a palazzo. Like mica,
the flock of turquoise reflects
light and flies into silvered
fields. Sagebrush seething.
I wonder how to fashion
bracelets of charms from the Milky Way.
Turn to my catalog of disorder,
sort new specimens collected
over the years. Devise in my dreams
a periodical table of agitation.
And became distracted
when the Earth tilted
away from light
and the sun dove into the dark sea.
Of course, the full moon rose
a bit akimbo, its arch barely
visible above the teeth
of mountain peaks
and spun overhead
into the theatre of stars.
The blue mountains turned
blood red, a miracle
that brought conquistadors
to their knees.

Landscape with Extraction

How they honeycomb the plains
with storage tanks, with new excavated
evaporation ponds, with white pipe snaking
over farmland to connect to gathering stations,
as the new crop sprouts
green the trenches open
near edges of cities
next to developments of prefab houses
two tall towers appear like my brother's erector
set or the dubious carnivals with their ferris wheel
assemble in ragtag strip mall
parking lots and materialize unannounced overnight.

Invasive monoliths parse and part
out the earth as if it were a carcass. Each
structure a dot on a journalist's map
blacking out all the counties to the Kansas
border. And into the earth's arteries the hypodermic
needle plunges deep. The hydraulic
whine supersedes the song of meadowlarks
and I heard today benzene is falling from the sky,
off-cuff, a notice hidden deep in the newspaper,
a revelation whispered.

And we are deep
in drought, the adjacent forest a tinderbox,
while the platoon of water trucks swarm
and hum like drones in a hive
and wait in line as this procedure requires
at least an ocean. The drilling occurs despite
our anxiety, the extraction of minerals
part of our heritage and as with dialysis
machines infuse sand, water and proprietary
chemicals deep into shale.

The West still mineral rich
this new boom and bust, still manifest
destiny, still all about scar and extraction,
still split estate and one morning
the outdoor factory can appear
on anyone's land set up shop,

and we are just collateral damage,
an afterthought. Another structure
appears imperial, impervious
and stampedes of flatbeds
loaded with pipe, water trucks, and earthmoving
equipment construct a new world.
We tend our backyard gardens
and surveyors urbanize an alien
universe

Heron & Bark

Rumors of bear send many back to the city
and multitudes miss the blue heron crouched low by the river
solo and silent waiting for fish.
Before long, our hearing will be out of tune with water
and our offspring grows tone deaf
to it rushing downstream.
Today the river is furious, overburdened by rainstorms
and is it always like this ~ as changeable as sky?
One morning the river turns indigo and silver,
fog rises breath above the cryptic surface,
then a smooth plate of glass inches downriver.
For me, forests are the perfect lyceum
where pine branches sprout clipped wings of large angels,
their feathers of bark lay askew on the ground
and midstream a quick flash of deer
sprints skittish out of view.
Yes, we are ambivalent about our expulsion
from the garden, but dry leaves rattle hymns to the wind
clear evidence this is still Eden
where everything happens for the very first time.

Benzene Spill, Sand Creek, Denver

Benzene, benign, benevolent at the turn of the last century
once an ingredient in men's aftershave,
nicknamed frankincense of Java for its seductive smell,
attractive to the opposite sex,
in the recipe for soda, in the formulary for Sanka.
Benzene once stocked in quart cans in hardware stores,
handled by students measuring out millimeters
for science experiments.
And yes the refinery
fell short, spills enough carcinogens to fill an Olympic-size pool
into a silence until a fly fisherman on the South Platte
gagged on the smell of oily sheen
the weird milky sludge clogged
upswells and mircocurrents
stilling some sixty carp
alive, but not very active and blogged.
Benzene, so carcinogenic
so regulated, a flume fans out
and seeps into groundwater
and yes, Suncor fell short of its commitment
to the city and only after the blog went viral
my flies smelled like gas, my hands smelled like gas
did they send a cavalry of cleanup crews
resplendent in white
biohazard suits skimming the water.

On Viewing *The First Photograph of the Atom Bomb,*
Trinity Test Site: July 16th 1945 5:25:45 A.M.

Today I saw the first photograph of the atom bomb,
enlarged, wallpapered on an entire wall of the New Mexico
Museum of Art surrounded by divisions.
Each art movement forward
was a kind of violence, an advancement, the swift
dismissal of the past, the word classical
an indictment, as the round forms for forearms,
thighs, the full moon of our faces flattened
until bodies disappear all together.
The pursuit of the new imagines the world
is nonrepresentational and we are all a series
of color fields.
Each painting is only conquest.

The black and white photograph is the most beautiful
object in the museum. More compelling than Clovis
points, arrow heads flicked into shape
fourteen thousand years ago killers of mastodons
or *retablos* and altars of saints, objects
of pure devotion and instigators of rosaries.

Point zero twenty-five seconds, the atom bomb
opens up like a parachute, a thin silk skin shimmers
a transparent jellyfish floating in the negative sea hovers over
desert promising the end of war and for a moment
almost beautiful, almost benevolent. A rumble froths
near the Earth's surface into a skirt of ruffles
for less than a split second luminous.

It is all about conquest, the moment before,
the moment after
as in, this oil painting of a missionary preaching to the Aztec king
and behind his back a phalanx of conquistadors
available for persuasion if the new voice
of god goes unheeded.

Now the birth of modernity,
the movement towards abstraction
which overtakes art in a sort
of manifest destiny, something I learned
in fifth grade as a positive force.
We live in uneasy peace as atomic
bombs and invasive plants from Europe
coexist. Everywhere on Earth ice is melting.

I have forgotten most objects the curator museumed
and deemed worthy of an afternoon's regard
still on my mind only black and white and the loss of all innocence.
None of these impulses will matter no paint smeared,
no reed woven, no clay fired could survive the blast.